Summer

Arrangements
from the
Southern Garden

I'M IN
THE GARDEN

Summer

Arrangements
from the
Southern Garden

Floral Design and Text by
Ralph Null

Photography by
Greg Campbell

Harmony House Publishers

Harmony House Publishers - Louisville
P.O. Box 90 Prospect Kentucky 40059
502.228.2010
©2002 Ralph Null
All rights reserved
Printed in Hong Kong
Executive Editor - William Strode
Book Design - Karen Boone
Library of Congress Control Number: 2002104834
ISBN 1-56469-091-1

Other Books by the Author

SPRING ARRANGEMENTS FROM
THE SOUTHERN GARDEN
by Ralph Null

CHRISTMAS COLLECTIONS
by Ralph Null and Bob Hampton

These books are available from
Design Concepts
P.O. Box 8707
Columbus MS 39705-0013
(662) 328-7741

Acknowledgments

The opportunity to collect flowers and foliage from many
private home gardens has added to the diversity of plant
materials and greatly enhanced the joy of doing this book
of summer floral designs. These gardens include those
of Martha and Frank Leigh, Charlie McCorkle, Barbara
Hodges, Putt Burris, Beth Sims, Rachel George, and Walter
McKay. Ruth and Scott Berry, Suzanne and Hunt Cade,
and Merriam and Ebner Etheridge not only opened their
gardens but also their homes and pools for photography.
Quite memorable are those fabulous tomato sandwiches at
the Etheridge's. Those old fashion variety tomatoes were
fresh picked from the most beautiful vegetable garden
that I have ever seen.

Greg Campbell's photography and willingness to get the
right shots when the flowers were available greatly enhance
this book. William Strode and Joe Paul Pruett make sure
that the end product is as beautiful as the flowers. And
especially to Fred Kinder who makes sure that everything
stays organized and that the books get distributed. To all
of you I want to say thank you for making this book possible.

*T*he summer garden in the south is both a joy and a tribulation. After the cool weather of a prolonged springtime, summer arrives and overnight an unbelievable blast of hot air descends, the air drips with humidity, the soil turns bone dry. Then every insect in the world arrives to see what's going on in your world. For the avid gardener this creates the constant need to water, spray, pluck, weed, prune, mulch, and pray for marginal success. The mildew, cutworms, blight, moles, rabbits, deer and drought are commonplace and we must face them every day that we enjoy the garden. Trying to grow all those beautiful things that we see in the magazines, whether its an English garden, or a western garden, a Japanese garden, or an old fashioned southern garden, it is important to understand the limitations of your own garden's location, soil, zone, and general environment. Don't let the beautiful pictures in books and magazines give you false hopes. Learn what works best in your own area and this will give you the best results.

Subscribe to everything, read everything, and then visit with a successful gardener in your own area and see what really works where you live. A visit to the big plant nursery at your local mass market is not the place where you decide at an instant what you want to plant throughout your garden plan. What looks so good in that nursery pot and compels you to buy will often never respond well in your own garden. Occasionally you will be joyously surprised but more frequently you will be disappointed. If you want a garden that requires minimal maintenance, visit an old cemetery, a neglected park, or an old home place and see what has thrived despite neglect. This is a sure indicator of plant hardiness.

The whole purpose of planning and planting a garden is to enjoy the beauty that it creates around you, to be able to cut flowers and foliage for use in the home, and to spend time communing with the earth while getting great exercise. This enjoyment is enhanced when these objectives are well balanced. When the work overcomes the enjoyment the enthusiasm can be greatly diminished.

Summer is a great time to use foliage in designs for the home, porch, or patio. They are generally long lasting and can withstand the summer heat for outside affairs. When a design is primarily composed of foliage, a few flowers can be used as an accent. An arrangement of greenery helps to create a feeling of coolness. With all the variations of color available in foliage, dramatic interest can be created.

Perhaps the most important thing to know when planning summer arrangements is who has what blooming in their garden. Gardeners love to share as is evidenced by many of the designs in this book. The roadsides, woodlands, vacant lots, and country fields are also great places to gather floral and foliage materials.

It is best to collect your materials early in the day while the temperatures are cooler. When collecting materials for your designs, you should take a bucket of water with you. Immediately put the cut materials into water. Summer heat quickly wilts cut materials. Place the cut materials in a cool place until you are ready to design with them.

Summer entertaining is often done outside and the use of natural materials is a good choice. A more casual style and simple arrangements are often best. I think that your arrangements should reflect your own personality and sense of style. Differing types of occasions will require different types of designs. In this book there are many different ideas and I hope that some of them will appeal to you and that you will be inspired to make your own summer arrangements with "southern style" from your garden.

ontents

For Entertaining

A simple basket, filled to overflowing with zinnias of every color, is the perfect choice for casual summer entertaining.

The Old Rose Advisor   Dickerson

ANTIQUE ROSES for the SOUTH

Landscaping with Antique Roses   Druitt and Shoup

A massive, colorful,

collection of garden blossoms

including hollyhocks, salvia,

daylilies, honeysuckle, phlox,

Irish eyes, hydrangea, and

oriental lilies, brighten this

living room table.

*P*okeberry and

chartreuse coleus fills

a Chinese footbath

with unusual color

and texture. Natural

materials can be

used with garden

flowers or foliage for

exciting contrast.

*C*risp, cool green and white is a perfect combination for summer flower arrangements.

*G*roups of flowers of a kind are placed in this export bowl. It makes the segmented design look as if were planted instead of being made of cut materials.

*D*ahlias,
verbena,
Goldquelle,
pokeberry,
spray roses,
and phlox
make a casual
country style
design.

*T*his basket of
garden delights
includes mosses,
ferns, grasses,
lichens, foliage,
assorted collected
blossoms, and a pair
of ceramic birds.

A colorful
soup tureen
is filled with
bigleaf, Peegee,
and Annabelle
hydrangea.

*C*rape myrtle
blooms all summer
and comes in many
colors. When it
has been properly
hydrated after
cutting, it will last
for several days
in a design.

Small
& Simple

A few garden roses, phlox, and hydrangea give warmth and interest to this conversation area.

LETTS GUIDES TO GARDEN DESIGN • GARDEN DESIGN • Cottage Garden • ELIZABETH PETER

• LETTS GUIDES TO GARDEN DESIGN • Cottage Garden • ELIZABETH ARTI

MARY TONETTI DORRA   BEAUTIFUL AMERICAN ROSE GA

VISIONS OF ROSES *by* PETER BEALE

Pots filled with open blossoms of antique garden roses line the center of the table. This is a great way to use short stemmed flowers yet it is elegant and aids in across-the-table conversation at a dinner party.

*S*alvia,
black-eyed
Susans, mini-
zinnias, and
hosta foliage
have been
casually dropped
into a lined
pine straw
basket.

*I*t only takes
one water lily to
be spectacular.

*A few
perfect, colorful
rose blossoms
accent this
coffee table.*

*A bowl of
colorful garden
peppers and
a single coneflower
brighten this
kitchen counter.*

Baby roses, dianthus, abelia, and celosia make a charming combination in this miniature trophy urn.

Nothing is more beautiful than this luscious bouquet of antique roses from the garden.

Creatively Natural

A wreath basket holds an interesting mixture of foliage, pods, seed heads, and fruits on the gate at the vegetable garden entrance.

A terra cotta pot wallhanger, filled with daisies, salvia, oregano, fern, and mint, adds interest to the garden fence.

Old fashioned flowers and foliage are accented with a dramatic use of coleus and hydrangea.

A welcome entry to the garden is expressed with a wall vase filled with French marigolds, trumpet vine, dusty miller, and andromeda.

Tradition requires a magnolia arrangement. These blossoms are from a Little Gem magnolia, which blooms almost all year and is of a size and scale well suited for the smaller garden and works well in floral designs.

Casual Elegance

*Salvia,
Mexican petunia,
coleus, lilies, and
obedient plant
create a colorful
centerpiece for
a porch table.*

A flowers-by-the-yard container is used to create a design that appears to be growing.

Dahlias remind me of my childhood. I often helped my aunt gather those big old-fashioned lavender dahlias from her garden and then we would make arrangements for Sunday church services.

Green zinnias, blue sage, hydrangea, sedum, dusty miller, liriope, ribbon grass, and maidenhair fern are combined for a surprising summer combination.

A few flowers dropped into a bottle collection make a stunning flower accent. This is an easy way to design and makes a few flowers look very effective.

A garden mix of foxglove, ageratum, buddleia, salvia, Queen Ann's lace, vitex, godetia, veronica, and lily grass creates a classical style summer garden design.

44

Coreopsis, zinnias, amaranthus, hosta, lamb's ear, citronella, and sage are a perfect accent on this coffee table.

Nothing says summer more than big, bold sunflowers and their garden companions.

Collections

Perfect peppers lying across Mexican glasses hold the flowers in place. The flower stems are inserted through the peppers and into the water below.

Ceramic vegetables on a tray hold specimen blossoms of salvia, rudbeckia, roses, and verbena.

Simply zinnias!

Poolside Entertaining

Crisp foliage makes a perfect summer cooler.

This floating wreath of assorted summer flowers is the perfect accent for a pool party.

An all-green arrangement of ginger, hydrangea, caladium, euphorbia, and cattail foliage is a cool design for a hot pool party.

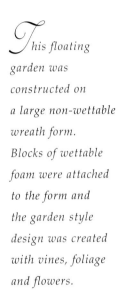

This floating garden was constructed on a large non-wettable wreath form. Blocks of wettable foam were attached to the form and the garden style design was created with vines, foliage and flowers.

Garden Bounty

Sunflowers, potato vine, crocosmia, and yucca pods fill a vase that is accessorized with a basket of Osage oranges and a chocolate geranium rosette.

Bell pepper topiaries with pablano pepper stems frame an arrangement of daylilies, garden lilies, artemisia, and camellia fruit. The topiaries are constructed on steel rods fitted into a heavy metal base.

Nerine lilies are dramatic in the garden and are equally dramatic in this design. They have been combined with calla foliage, phlox, red basil, and wedding fern.

Nothing is more beautiful than a bountiful collection of vibrant flowers and colorful vegetables.

Summer riches!